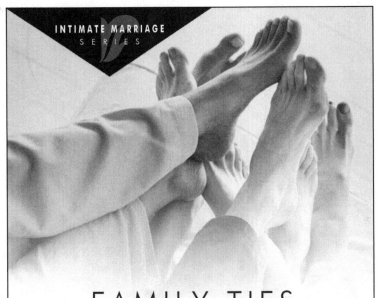

INTIMATE MARRIAGE
S E R I E S

FAMILY TIES

Dan B. Allender
and Tremper Longman III

6 STUDIES FOR INDIVIDUALS, COUPLES OR GROUPS

InterVarsity Press
Downers Grove, Illinois

InterVarsity Press
P.O. Box 1400, Downers Grove, IL 60515-1426
World Wide Web: www.ivpress.com
E-mail: mail@ivpress.com

InterVarsity Press® is the book-publishing division of InterVarsity Christian Fellowship/USA®, a student
movement active on campus at hundreds of universities, colleges and schools of nursing in the United States
of America, and a member movement of the International Fellowship of Evangelical Students. For
information about local and regional activities, write Public Relations Dept., InterVarsity Christian
Fellowship/USA, 6400 Schroeder Rd., P.O. Box 7895, Madison, WI 53707-7895, or visit the IVCF website
at <www.intervarsity.org>.

Design: Cindy Kiple

Images: Martin Barraud/Getty Images

ISBN 0-8308-2135-X

Printed in the United States of America ∞

P	18	17	16	15	14	13	12	11	10	9	8	7	6	5	4	3	2	1
Y	18	17	16	15	14	13	12	11	10	09	08	07	06	05				

CONTENTS

Welcome to Intimate Marriage Bible Studies 5

1 FAMILY TRADITIONS 9
   Exodus 12:1-16; Matthew 26:17-30

2 FAMILY STORIES 17
   Deuteronomy 6:20-25; Psalm 78:1-8

3 FAMILY TRAUMAS 24
   2 Samuel 12:1-16; Philippians 3:12-14

4 FAMILY COMPARISONS 31
   Genesis 37:2-8

5 FAMILY LEGALISM 37
   Colossians 2:14-23

6 A SPIRITUAL LEGACY 43
   Selections from Proverbs

Leader's Notes 48

113718

INTIMATE MARRIAGE

FAMILY TIES

Marriages don't exist in a vacuum. We are born in a family, we marry into a family, and we die in the context of a family. "Blood is thicker than water" is not a biblical proverb, but the Bible does talk about the importance of family. Families bring joy and pain, both our families of origin as well as the families that our marriages produce.

The following studies look at biblical passages that help us understand the effect that family ties have on our marriages. Our desire is to steer clear of those that negatively affect the growth and enjoyment of marriage and to embrace those that enrich our lives together. We desire to draw on the best of our upbringing in order to create a context in our own marriages and families that will leave an enduring and positive spiritual legacy for the generations that will follow us.

TAKING MARRIAGE SERIOUSLY

Most of us want to have a good marriage. Those who don't have a good relationship yearn for a better one, and those who have a good one want even more intimacy.

We want to know our spouse and be known by them. We want

to be loved and to love. In short, we want the type of marriage desired by God from the beginning when he created the institution of marriage and defined it as involving leaving parents, weaving a life of intimacy together and cleaving in sexual bliss.

These studies delve into the wisdom of the Bible in order to learn what it takes to have not just a "good" marriage but one that enjoys the relational richness that God intended for a husband and a wife. This divinely instituted type of marriage is one that will

- Bring a husband and wife closer together
- Understand that marriage is one's primary loyalty to other human beings
- Be characterized by a growing love and knowledge of one another
- Be an arena of spiritual growth
- Allow for the healthy exposure of sin through the offer of forgiveness
- Be a crucible for showing grace
- Reflect God's love for his people
- Enjoy God's gift of sexual intimacy
- Share life's joys and troubles
- Have a part in transforming us from sinners to saints
- Bring out each other's glory as divine image bearers

And so much more! The Bible provides a wealth of insight, and these studies hope to tap its riches and bring them to bear on our marriage relationships.

USING THE STUDIES

These studies can be used in a variety of contexts—individual devotional life, by a couple together or by a small group—or in a combination of these settings. Each study includes the following components.

Open. Several quotes at the beginning give a sense of what married people say about the topic at hand. These are followed by a question that can be used for discussion. If you are using the DVD, you may want to skip this and go straight to the opening clip.

DVD Reflection. For each session we have an opening thought from Dan Allender, at times accompanied by an excerpt from our interviews with married couples, to get you thinking about the topic at hand. This material will provide fresh and engaging openers for a small group as well as interesting discussion points for couples studying together. You will find a question here to discuss after you watch the DVD clip.

Study. One or more key Bible texts are included in the guide for convenience. We have chosen the New Living Translation, but you may use any version of Scripture you like. The questions in this section will take you through the key aspects of the passage and help you apply them to your marriage. Sprinkled throughout the study, you will also find commentary to enrich your experience.

For the Couple. Here's an opportunity to make an application and commitment, which is specific to your marriage.

Bonus. These are further ideas for study on your own. Or if you are studying with a group, take time to do the bonus item with your spouse during the week.

We hope that these studies enrich your marriage. We encourage you to be brutally honest with yourself and tactfully honest with your spouse. If you are willing to be honest with yourself and with the Scripture, then God will do great things for your marriage. That is our prayer.

FAMILY TRADITIONS

"Every Easter Julie reads the story of Christ's crucifixion and resurrection from the Gospel of John. We don't do Easter egg hunts. That way we put the day in its proper setting."

"We don't celebrate Christmas, because it really is just a pagan holiday that early Christians covered over, and now it's so commercialized."

"Traditions! The Pharisees had traditions! We worship God in spirit and truth, spontaneously."

"Every full moon we have some friends over. We call it a 'New Moon party.' There is nothing astrological about it; it's just that the light of the moon sets a certain mood."

▶ OPEN

Establishing family traditions can be tricky. Newly married couples often struggle with how they will relate to the traditions of their parents. Will they continue to have Christmas with Mom and Dad, or will they have their own celebration? While the Bible does not answer such questions with a clear yes or no, our study will suggest that traditions are important because memory plays a crucial role in the Christian faith. What different traditions do you bring to your marriage?

▶ DVD REFLECTION

What different expectations about family relationships do you bring to your marriage?

▶ STUDY

Read Exodus 12:1-16.

While the Israelites were still in the land of Egypt, the LORD gave the following instructions to Moses and Aaron: [2]"From now on, this month will be the first month of the year for you. [3]Announce to the whole community of Israel that on the tenth day of this month each family must choose a lamb or a young goat for a sacrifice, one animal for each household. [4]If a family is too small to eat a whole animal, let them share with another family in the neighborhood. Divide the animal according to the size of each family and how much they can eat. [5]The animal you select must be a one-year-old male, either a sheep or a goat, with no defects.

[6]"Take special care of this chosen animal until the evening of the fourteenth day of this first month. Then the whole assembly of the community of Israel must slaughter their lamb or young goat at twilight. [7]They are to take some of the blood and smear it on the sides and top of the doorframes of the houses where they eat the animal. [8]That same night they must roast the meat over a fire and eat it along with bitter salad greens and bread made without yeast. [9]Do not eat any of the meat raw or boiled in water. The

whole animal—including the head, legs, and internal organs— must be roasted over a fire. [10]Do not leave any of it until the next morning. Burn whatever is not eaten before morning.

[11]"These are your instructions for eating this meal: Be fully dressed, wear your sandals, and carry your walking stick in your hand. Eat the meal with urgency, for this is the LORD's Passover. [12]On that night I will pass through the land of Egypt and strike down every firstborn son and firstborn male animal in the land of Egypt. I will execute judgment against all the gods of Egypt, for I am the LORD! [13]But the blood on your doorposts will serve as a sign, marking the houses where you are staying. When I see the blood, I will pass over you. This plague of death will not touch you when I strike the land of Egypt.

[14]"This is a day to remember. Each year, from generation to generation, you must celebrate it as a special festival to the LORD. This is a law for all time. [15]For seven days the bread you eat must be made without yeast. On the first day of the festival, remove every trace of yeast from your homes. Anyone who eats bread made with yeast during the seven days of the festival will be cut off from the community of Israel. [16]On the first day of the festival and again on the seventh day, all the people must observe an official day for holy assembly. No work of any kind may be done on these days except in the preparation of food."

Read Matthew 26:17-30.

On the first day of the Festival of Unleavened Bread, the disciples came to Jesus and asked, "Where do you want us to prepare the Passover meal for you?"

[18]"As you go into the city," he told them, "you will see a certain man. Tell him, 'The Teacher says: My time has come, and I
will eat the Passover meal with my disciples at your house.'"
[19]So the disciples did as Jesus told them and prepared the Passover meal there.

[20]When it was evening, Jesus sat down at the table with the
twelve disciples.[21] While they were eating, he said, "I tell you the
truth, one of you will betray me."

[22]Greatly distressed, each one asked in turn, "Am I the one,
Lord?"

[23]He replied, "One of you who has just eaten from this bowl
with me will betray me. [24]For the Son of Man must die, as the
Scriptures declared long ago. But how terrible it will be for the
one who betrays him. It would be far better for that man if he had
never been born!"

[25]Judas, the one who would betray him, also asked, "Rabbi, am
I the one?"

And Jesus told him, "You have said it."

[26]As they were eating, Jesus took some bread and blessed it.
Then he broke it in pieces and gave it to the disciples, saying,
"Take this and eat it, for this is my body."

[27]And he took a cup of wine and gave thanks to God for it. He
gave it to them and said, "Each of you drink from it, [28]for this is
my blood, which confirms the covenant between God and his
people. It is poured out as a sacrifice to forgive the sins of many.
[29]Mark my words—I will not drink wine again until the day I
drink it new with you in my Father's Kingdom."

[30]Then they sang a hymn and went out to the Mount of Olives.

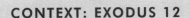

CONTEXT: EXODUS 12

Exodus 12, which both describes the first Passover celebration and establishes the annual tradition, comes at the climax of the account of the plagues with which God has afflicted Egypt, beginning with turning the water of the Nile into blood. The final horrific plague resulted in the death of firstborn sons among the Egyptians and their animals. The result was a great victory over the "gods of Egypt" (see Exodus 12:12). After this, the Egyptians allowed the Israelites to leave their bondage. Though they would change their minds and try vainly to stop the Israelites at the Red Sea, it was the aftermath of the twelfth plague that was seen as the point when Israel gained its freedom. Thus God directed Israel to observe an annual Passover ceremony to remind them of his great act of salvation.

1. Exodus 12 recounts the establishment of the annual celebration of Passover, and Matthew 26 the establishment of the Last Supper. What event does each of these commemorate?

2. Have you ever celebrated Passover? If so, how did it affect you?

3. What is the relationship between Passover and Communion?

4. What are family traditions?

Sometimes we associate these traditions with children, but traditions are important for all couples. What are some traditions that work well for couples?

5. How can traditions be helpful to establishing family unity?

How can they help spiritual growth?

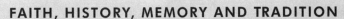

FAITH, HISTORY, MEMORY AND TRADITION
The Judeo-Christian religion is deeply rooted in history. It teaches and strongly depends on the reality of God's redemptive actions in space and time. For this reason, memory plays a large role in faith. We look to the past for our confidence in the present and hope for the future. Our memory is bolstered by traditions that preserve the stories of past redemptions.

How could they hurt unity or growth?

6. What are some helpful nonreligious celebrations?

7. Should traditions be focused within the nuclear family, or are there benefits to having the extended family involved as well?

8. Tell about some traditions that your family observes each year.

▶ FOR THE COUPLE

Sit down and think about your year together. Are there certain traditions that you always observe?

What do you cherish about these times?

What would happen to you personally and corporately if these times were not part of your life?

How do you go about creating special traditions?

Are there others that you would want to establish? Why or why not?

▶ BONUS

God established the tradition of animal sacrifice in ancient Israel to symbolize atonement for sins, among other things. Read Micah 6:6-8. Why does God take such a negative view of Israel's sacrifices here?

2

FAMILY STORIES

"It's such a shame. I don't know anything about my family line. My grandparents died when I was young, and my parents never talk about them."

"It's incredibly encouraging to me to know that our faith has been passed down for at least the past two generations."

"When I heard about my grandparents, I felt I understood my mother better."

"I love to talk to my kids about what Jesus did for us."

▶ OPEN

When someone asks us a question about ourselves, we respond with a story—that is, if we are willing to expose ourselves beyond a simple one-word answer. "Where were you born?" "Where did you go to college?" "When did you first meet?" "Do you have any children?"

Our faith is also story-based. "When did you become a Christian?" "Why do you believe?" "What is the good news?"

Intimate marriages and strong families are built on a willingness to share stories. We reveal ourselves and our faith to our spouse and our children by telling each other stories about the past. How well do you know your spouse, and how well does your spouse know you?

▶ DVD REFLECTION

Reflecting on the DVD, how have you found that family stories affect a marriage?

▶ STUDY

Read Deuteronomy 6:20-25.

[20]"In the future your children will ask you, 'What is the meaning of these laws, decrees, and regulations that the LORD our God has commanded us to obey?'

[21]"Then you must tell them, 'We were Pharaoh's slaves in Egypt, but the LORD brought us out of Egypt with his strong hand. [22]The LORD did miraculous signs and wonders before our eyes, dealing terrifying blows against Egypt and Pharaoh and all his people. [23]He brought us out of Egypt so he could give us this land he had sworn to our ancestors. [24]And the LORD our God commanded us to obey all these decrees and to fear him so he can continue to bless us and preserve our lives, as he has done to this day. [25]For we will be counted as righteous when we obey all the commands the LORD our God has given us.'"

Read Psalm 78:1-8.

[1]O my people, listen to my instructions.
[2] Open your ears to what I am saying,

for I will speak to you in a parable.
I will teach you hidden lessons from our past—
³ stories we have heard and known
   stories our ancestors handed down to us.
⁴We will not hide these truths from our children;
   we will tell the next generation
about the glorious deeds of the LORD,
   about his power and his mighty wonders.
⁵For he issues his laws to Jacob;
   he gave his instructions to Israel.
He commanded our ancestors
   to teach them to their children,
⁶so the next generation might know them—
   even the children not yet born—
   and they in turn will teach their own children.
⁷So each generation should set its hope anew on God,
   not forgetting his glorious miracles
   and obeying his commands.
⁸Then they will not be like their ancestors—
   stubborn, rebellious, and unfaithful,
   refusing to give their hearts to God. (Psalm 78:1-8)

1. In Deuteronomy 6, what do the children ask their parents to tell them about the past?

Why do you think they are asking?

2. How do the parents respond to their children's question?

Why?

3. Do you remember wanting to hear stories about your own family when you were young?

If so, what was one of your favorites?

4. According to Psalm 78, why should one generation tell another about God's acts in the past?

CONTEXT: PSALM 78

Verses 1-8 make up the first stanza of one of the longest psalms in the book (72 verses). After announcing his intention to tell the next generation about God's actions in history, the psalmist recounts events that go back to the exodus, the crossing of the Red Sea and the wilderness wanderings. He reminds the people of God's redemptive acts in light of the fact that they have sinned against God, particularly during the reign of Saul. The poem ends with great hope, however, announcing the choice of David as king and of Zion as the place where his sanctuary will be located.

5. Throughout the Old Testament, the family is the primary means of passing on the stories of the faith. In the New Testament, the church, often described as a family, is mentioned more often than the family as the place where people recount the great stories of redemption. What do you think that tells us today?

6. What are stories of faith?

stories of hope?

stories of love?

Talk about the differences between these kinds of stories and what each might bring to your marriage.

▼

"I WILL SPEAK TO YOU IN A PARABLE"

The psalmist announces that he will speak to the people in a parable (78:2), so we are surprised when he goes on to recount events that happened in history. By calling the story of Israel's relationship with God a parable, he is not denying that it actually happened. However, he is making clear that he is interested in more than reporting facts. He desires to bring out the meaning of the facts. What significance does the exodus have for the people in their present situation?

7. Why should we share faith stories with each other in our families and church communities?

8. Where do we get the stories to tell each other?

▶ FOR THE COUPLE

Do you talk about God together often as a couple, as a family?

Does it come naturally, or does it feel forced?

Is your talk about God reserved to certain times and certain subjects? If so, why?

The foundational stories of Christians come from the Bible itself. Do you study Scripture?

Do you read it alone, together as a couple, together as a family?

Review your commitment to know God through Scripture. Devise a strategy, if necessary, to commit yourself to learn the Bible.

▶ BONUS

If you are working through this study in a group, have every couple take a turn telling a story about God's faithfulness in their married life.

3

FAMILY TRAUMAS

"I think he loves me. But after my father betrayed my mother, I can't quite trust any man."

"Life is full of risks. I know the danger of surrender and commitment, but the alternative is a lonely existence."

"Whenever I think of doing something stupid like that, I think of the ramifications for my family, and so far it has kept me from acting on the temptation."

"My parents were truly messed up relationally. If I think about it much, it paralyzes me. However, since I have become a Christian, I have been able to forgive and move forward."

▶ OPEN

Not all family stories are pleasant and encouraging. Most people can look to their past and remember painful experiences. Perhaps a tired and angry father hit his son too hard, or a neglected mother took it out on her children by being brutally demanding. Maybe one's parents were alcoholic and abusive, or a relative was sexually abusive over a period of years. Such a history can have significant repercussions in one's present marriage and family dynamics. How can the past sins of others affect how we treat people today?

▶ DVD REFLECTION

Do you agree that keeping family secrets harms a marriage? Why or why not?

▶ STUDY

In this study we will explore some of the effects of family trauma in the life of David.

Read 2 Samuel 12:1-16.

So the LORD sent Nathan the prophet to tell David this story: "There were two men in a certain town. One was rich, and one was poor. ²The rich man owned a great many sheep and cattle. ³The poor man owned nothing but one little lamb he had bought. He raised that little lamb, and it grew up with his children. It ate from the man's own plate and drank from his cup. He cuddled it in his arms like a baby daughter. ⁴One day a guest arrived at the home of the rich man. But instead of killing an animal from his own flock or herd, he took the poor man's lamb and killed it and prepared it for his guest."

⁵David was furious. "As surely as the LORD lives," he vowed, "any man who would do such a thing deserves to die! ⁶He must repay four lambs to the poor man for the one he stole and for having no pity."

⁷Then Nathan said to David, "You are that man! The LORD, the

God of Israel, says: I anointed you king of Israel and saved you from the power of Saul. [8]I gave you your master's house and his wives and the kingdoms of Israel and Judah. And if that had not been enough, I would have given you much, much more. [9]Why, then, have you despised the word of the LORD and done this horrible deed? For you have murdered Uriah the Hittite with the sword of the Ammonites and stolen his wife. [10]From this time on, your family will live by the sword because you have despised me by taking Uriah's wife to be your own.

[11]"This is what the LORD says: Because of what you have done, I will cause your own household to rebel against you. I will give your wives to another man before your very eyes, and he will go to bed with them in public view. [12]You did it secretly, but I will make this happen to you openly in the sight of all Israel.' "

[13]Then David confessed to Nathan, "I have sinned against the LORD."

Nathan replied, "Yes, but the LORD has forgiven you, and you won't die for this sin. [14]Nevertheless, because you have shown utter contempt for the LORD by doing this, your child will die."

[15]After Nathan returned to his home, the LORD sent a deadly illness to the child of David and Uriah's wife.

Read Philippians 3:12-14.

[12]I don't mean to say that I have already achieved these things or that I have already reached perfection. But I press on to possess that perfection for which Christ Jesus first possessed me. [13]No, dear brothers and sisters, I have not achieved it, but I focus on this one thing: Forgetting the past and looking forward to what lies

ahead, [14]I press on to reach the end of the race and receive the heavenly prize for which God, through Christ Jesus, is calling us.

1. Why do you think Nathan took an indirect approach by telling David the story about the rich man who stole a sheep from a poor man?

What does his approach tell you about sin?

CONTEXT: DAVID AND BATHSHEBA

At a time "when kings normally go out to war" (2 Samuel 11:1), David was on his roof and saw the naked Bathsheba taking a bath. He decided to sleep with her, and when he did, she got pregnant. David now had a problem, which he tried to resolve by calling her husband Uriah the Hittite back from the front line and encouraging him to relax. He hoped that Uriah would sleep with his wife and, when he learned of the pregnancy, assume the child was his. However, Uriah was unwilling to sleep with his wife while the rest of the army was in the midst of battle.

Since David's attempt at covering up his sin of adultery had not worked, he arranged for Uriah's death on the battlefield. In this way David compounded the sin of adultery with the sin of murder.

2. What consequences are predicted for David as a result of his sin?

Do you think the consequences are fair? Why or why not?

3. David confesses his guilt and repents (see also Psalm 51, a prayer of penitence connected to this episode). Does repentance automatically remove all negative effects of sin? Explain why or why not.

If not, then why repent?

4. If sin clearly has such negative consequences for ourselves and our family, why do we continue to sin?

THE CONSEQUENCES OF SIN

Once confronted by Nathan, David repented (see 2 Samuel 12:13-25; Psalm 51). However, though God forgave David, the consequences of his sin haunted him and his descendants for a long time to come. First, the child in Bathsheba's womb died soon after birth, and Nathan announced that this was because of David's sin (2 Samuel 12:14). In addition, the introduction of Bathsheba among the king's other wives triggered jealousies and power struggles that affected all of his descendants. Here is a sampling:

Amnon. This son of David, like his father, took a woman who did not belong to him. He raped his half-sister Tamar. For this he was murdered by Tamar's brother Absalom. Absalom. After murdering Amnon, Absalom was ostracized from his family, though David continued to love him. David allowed him to return, but on his return he fomented a rebellion against his father. After his initial success, David's army defeated him, and he was killed in a rather undignified manner as he fled. Adonijah. Toward the end of David's life, when he seemed too old to protest, Adonijah let himself be proclaimed king. However, it appears that David wanted his son Solomon to succeed him, so Adonijah was pushed out of the way by powerful forces in support of Solomon. Soon after Solomon assumed the throne, he found a pretext to have Adonijah killed. Solomon. Solomon was born to David and Bathsheba after their first child died. Solomon was in many ways the most promising of David's children. When he became king, he eagerly desired to follow God and lead his people well. However, he married women he shouldn't have, including the daughter of the Egyptian pharaoh. He soon began worshiping foreign gods and oppressing his own people. When he died, the kingdom was ripped in two.

5. How can adults who grew up in a troubled family avoid suffering the consequences of their parents' behavior?

6. How might Philippians 3:12-14 relate to past family trauma and its present effects?

7. Paul says he *forgot* his sinful past. Is this really possible?

▶ FOR THE COUPLE

Have you been honest with each other and with yourself in terms of the pains of the past? Why or why not?

Can you recognize present problems that arise from past abuses?

If you can, talk to each other about pain from the past. If necessary, get the help of a friend, a pastor or a counselor to work through some of these tough issues.

▶ BONUS

What are the different types of traumas that can leave lasting effects on families?

4

FAMILY COMPARISONS

"I will never forget the moment my mother told me that she pre-ferred my brother over me. She said she was compensating for my father's favoritism."

"My parents always treated my brother and me on an equal foot-ing. I plan to do the same with our children."

"Our oldest son is eager to please, but our middle son is high maintenance. I've got to give more time to him. As for the youngest, she has so many friends we hardly ever see her."

▶ OPEN

Consciously or not, sometimes a married couple will use their children as tools against each other. At other times a child will compensate parents for their marriage's lack of intimacy. What are some other ways that family dynamics affect a marriage?

▶ DVD REFLECTION

What are some of the differences in how your families of origin function?

▶ STUDY

The Bible includes a number of stories about sibling rivalry and its negative consequences for marriage and family, but none so compelling as the story of Joseph and his brothers

Read Genesis 37:2-8.

[2]This is the account of Jacob and his family. When Joseph was seventeen years old, he often tended his father's flocks. He worked for his half brothers, the sons of his father's wives Bilhah and Zilpah. But Joseph reported to his father some of the bad things his brothers were doing.

[3]Jacob loved Joseph more than any of his other children because Joseph had been born to him in his old age. So one day Jacob had a special gift made for Joseph—a beautiful robe. [4]But his brothers hated Joseph because their father loved him more than the rest of them. They couldn't say a kind word to him.

[5]One night Joseph had a dream, and when he told his brothers about it, they hated him more than ever. [6]"Listen to this dream," he said. [7]"We were out in the field, tying up bundles of grain. Suddenly my bundle stood up, and your bundles all gathered around and bowed low before mine!"

[8]His brothers responded, "So you think you will be our king, do you? Do you actually think you will reign over us?" And they hated him all the more because of his dreams and the way he talked about them.

1. What elements of rivalry and favoritism are at work in Joseph's family?

WHY IS JOSEPH THE FAVORITE CHILD?

The answer to this question is discovered in the chapters that precede the Joseph story (particularly Genesis 29:1—30:24). After a crisis caused by his sibling rivalry with Esau, Jacob fled to Paddan-Aram, where he fell in love with Rachel. Her father, Laban, said Jacob could marry Rachel if he worked for him for seven years. Jacob did so, but on his wedding night, Laban substituted Rachel's older sister Leah in her place. Jacob had to agree to work another seven years before he could wed Rachel. In other words, Rachel was the one he loved; Leah was forced on him.

This family dynamic kindled a baby war. Leah started having multiple babies, driving Rachel crazy. Rachel then provided a secondary wife for Jacob and through her had children, but Leah responded by giving Jacob her own choice of secondary wife. Finally, Rachel had her own child, Joseph. Later she had a second baby, Benjamin, but she died while giving birth to him.

When Joseph's story opens, he is the oldest child of the only woman Jacob really loved, who was now dead. While we cannot condone Jacob's favoritism, we can at least understand it.

2. How does his telling of his dream makes things worse?

3. What effects can children have on a marriage relationship?

4. Is it ever right to show partiality to one child over another? Explain.

CONTEXT: THE STORY OF JOSEPH

While the story of Joseph allows us to discuss family dynamics, that is not what Genesis 37—50 really about. Joseph himself articulates the theme of the story in Genesis 50:20. After his father Jacob dies, Joseph's brothers worry that Joseph will take revenge on them for their treatment of him. After all, they had sold him into slavery to get rid of him. However, Joseph recognizes the hand of God in his tumultuous life. "You intended to harm me, but God intended it all for good. He brought me to this position so I could save the lives of many people."

Joseph had been sold into slavery, falsely accused of rape and forgotten in an Egyptian prison. But God used each of these difficult things to bring him to a position of power in Egypt, so he could provide for his family, the family of the promise, during a devastating famine. The story of Joseph demonstrates how God overrules evil for good.

5. Aside from parental favoritism, what other dynamics can generate sibling comparisons and power struggles in a family?

6. What are the dangers that sibling comparisons and power struggles pose to a marriage?

7. How can parents prevent or defuse problems generated by power struggles among and with children?

with each other?

8. How should a couple handle the following situation? One parent feels strongly that a child is doing something for which he or she needs discipline, but the other parent disagrees equally strongly. They both think the well-being of the child is at stake.

▶ FOR THE COUPLE WITH CHILDREN

Talk together about the dynamic among your children. Do they all feel equally and fully loved?

Are there aspects of your relationships with your children that you would like to see changed?

How do the two of you handle conflict concerning childrearing issues?

▶ FOR THE COUPLE WITHOUT CHILDREN

It is never too early to start talking about these issues. Discuss and pray together about raising your children in ways that will minimize power struggles.

▶ BONUS

At the beginning of the story, the siblings all hate Joseph and seek to get rid of him. By the end of the story, after Jacob dies, Joseph is effectively the head of the family. What led to this new situation?

5

FAMILY LEGALISM

"My wife really puts the screws on me. I can't move without her noticing."

"My husband says we have to pray every day, that if we don't something bad might happen to us."

"I won't send my kid to that Christian college. They allow dances on campus and even drinking if they are over twenty-one."

▶ OPEN

Randy grew up in a church where he was told exactly what to do and what not to do. He could grow his hair only so long, and his sister had to wear dresses that covered her knees. As a result, today he struggles with any kind of authority and has difficulty going to church and reading the Bible.

We want to avoid such damaging legalism. Still, the Bible makes it clear that the Christian life does make demands and that certain forms of behavior and thought are more than out of bounds—they are repulsive to God himself. How can we cultivate family life that encourages both obedience and joy?

▶ DVD REFLECTION

What experiences have you had with legalism?

▶ STUDY

Perhaps our study in Colossians 2 will help us mediate the difference between legalism and wise living.

Read Colossians 2:14-23.

[14]He canceled the record of the charges against us and took it away by nailing it to the cross. [15]In this way he disarmed the spiritual rulers and authorities. He shamed them publicly by his victory over them on the cross.

[16]So don't let anyone condemn you for what you eat or drink, or for not celebrating certain holy days or new moon ceremonies or Sabbaths. [17]For these rules are only shadows of the reality yet to come. And Christ himself is that reality. [18]Don't let anyone condemn you by insisting on pious self-denial or the worship of angels, saying they have had visions about these things. Their sinful minds have made them proud, [19]and they are not connected to Christ, the head of the body. For he holds the whole body together with its joints and ligaments, and it grows as God nourishes it.

[20]You have died with Christ, and he has set you free from the spiritual powers of this world. So why do you keep on following the rules of the world, such as, [21]"Don't handle! Don't taste! Don't touch!"? [22]Such rules are mere human teaching about things that deteriorate as we use them. [23]These rules may seem wise because they

require strong devotion, pious self-denial, and severe bodily discipline. But they provide no help in conquering a person's evil desires.

1. Paul tells the Colossian Christians not to follow certain regulations. Why?

HUMAN LAWS

God has given human beings laws to live by for their own good. However, from time immemorial human beings have seen fit to add to God's laws. This is often called fencing the law, making rules that attempt to protect us from even getting close to breaking God's law. If we are not to take God's name in vain, we will never say the name of God, Yahweh. If we are not to be drunk, we will never drink alcohol. If we are not to have sex outside of marriage, we will never dance with a partner who is not our spouse. The list goes on and on. Even with the best intentions, though, such rule making involves human beings' attempts to act like God, and usually the consequences are unfortunate. It is dangerous to add to the Word of God.

2. Are there laws that God still wants us to follow today?

If so, how is this not legalism?

NEW TESTAMENT LEGALISM

The Old Testament was grace based from the start. Notice how the Ten Commandments are preceded by the statement "I am the LORD your God, who rescued you from slavery in Egypt" (Exodus 20:2). In other words, relationship with God precedes lawkeeping. People did not become followers of God by keeping the law, but they did maintain their relationship by keeping it.

However, by the time of the New Testament some of God's people put a higher premium on lawkeeping than the Old Testament itself did, and some of these legalistic ideas pervaded certain sectors of the church. Even Peter struggled with the role of law in the faith (Acts 10-11), and Paul had to confront him about it (Galatians 2:11-21).

Some leaders and teachers thought that certain aspects of the Old Testament law (such as circumcision) had to be observed even by Gentile believers in Jesus. Many of the New Testament epistles confront and condemn such legalism.

3. Is it legalistic to tell a young child not to cross the road without looking? Is it legalistic to request that your wife not spend too much time with another man whom you suspect has an inordinate interest in her? Is it wrong to confront a husband who is working twelve hours a day, six days a week? After all, none of these are breaking biblical "laws." Explain your response.

4. How can we tell the difference between a matter of law and a matter of wisdom?

5. How can we tell when the time is right to apply a principle of wisdom?

CONTEMPORARY LEGALISM

The gospel is good news of grace and freedom. We were once slaves to sin and the law, but Jesus has set us free. Paul speaks of us now as slaves to Jesus (1 Corinthians 7:22), but this is a slavery that gives us joy. We are not free to do whatever we want without consequences (Romans 6:1-14); we are free for righteousness. Then why do many people who grow up in a Christian household say that life in their family was dark and oppressive? Why do many Christian marriages seem unhappy? Some grew up experiencing the Christian life as one rule after another. In some marriages, the spouses' life together feels like duty rather than joy, fear rather than hope.

6. What effects does legalism have on people as they grow up?

as they get married?

7. Why do Christians tend to add to the law?

8. What are some examples of how married couples get legalistic with each other?

9. Is it ever appropriate for husbands and wives to make demands of each other? Explain.

▶ **FOR THE COUPLE**

Examine your marriage and the expectations and demands that you place on each other. Is yours a legalistic marriage or one where you seek each other's good?

▶ **BONUS**

What does a household look like in which the members live by grace and wisdom rather than by legalism? Imagine together what it would mean for a family to let go of legalism.

6

A SPIRITUAL LEGACY

"I am so grateful for what my parents taught me and what their parents taught them."

"No one in my family was a Christian, and I am very thankful for what God has done in my life. I want to raise my children in the faith."

"I'm very proud of my grandchildren."

▶ OPEN

Marriage is a union of two people in an intimate relationship. Contrary to some popular conceptions, marriage is not for the sole purpose of having children. Yet most marriages will lead to descendants. We get so caught up in the immediate moment that we forget the long-term, multigenerational influence of our lives, for good and for ill. Describe someone in your family (or in your spiritual family) who has left you a significant legacy.

▶ DVD REFLECTION

What legacy do you want your marriage to leave on those around you?

▶ STUDY

A number of biblical proverbs remind us of the legacy that can come from faithful lives and can motivate us to live our marriages faithfully in the present.

Read the following selections from Proverbs.

A youngster's heart is filled with foolishness,
  but discipline will drive it far away. (22:15)

Direct your children onto the right path,
  and when they are older, they will not leave it. (22:6)

The godly walk with integrity;
  blessed are their children who follow them. (20:7)

Evil people will surely be punished,
  but the children of the godly will go free. (11:21)

Grandchildren are the crowning glory of the aged;
  parents are the pride of their children. (17:6)

1. Proverbs 22:15 suggests that children are inherently foolish. If you have children, does this ring true?

2. Proverbs 22:15 insists that discipline is what is necessary to re- move foolishness from the heart of a child. What do you think *discipline* means here?

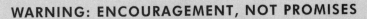

WARNING: ENCOURAGEMENT, NOT PROMISES

The proverbs we are studying encourage parents to be faithful in their teaching and role modeling. They motivate parents by reminding them that to do so is important and positive for their children. However, it is not in the nature of a proverb to make promises. Proverbs tell us what actions are likely to bring good consequences, but they do not offer guarantees. Other things being equal, it is much more likely that a child of a godly parent will grow up to live a godly life than a child who is neglected. In spite of one's efforts to train a child in the right way, however, that child may go wrong for other reasons. These proverbs can motivate us to teach our children well, but we may not use these proverbs to judge whether a parent has done an adequate job. The fact that a child goes bad does not mean that her or his parents are at fault.

3. Proverbs 22:6 encourages parents to direct their children onto "the right path." What is the right path?

4. Why are the children of those who walk in integrity blessed (20:7)?

5. According to Proverbs 11:21, why do the children of the godly go free?

How is that related to the punishment of evil people?

6. Proverbs 17:6 describes three generations of a family, each blessing the other. Does this always hold true?

7. Do we strive to have godly children, or are they a gift from God?

▶ **FOR THE COUPLE**

Think back to your parents and grandparents. What is their spiritual legacy in your lives?

Think forward to your children and grandchildren (born or yet to be born). What is the legacy you want to leave them?

What do you need to do to move toward that desired goal?

▶ BONUS

Ask to interview an older Christian couple about the legacy they have begun to see in their children and grandchildren. What can they tell you about discipline, modeling, parenting failures and the operation of God's grace?

LEADER'S NOTES

My grace is sufficient for you.

2 CORINTHIANS 12:9 NIV

Leading a Bible discussion can be an enjoyable and rewarding experience. But it can also be *scary*—especially if you've never done it before. If this is your feeling, you're in good company. When God asked Moses to lead the Israelites out of Egypt, he replied, "O Lord, please send someone else to do it" (Ex 4:13 NIV). It was the same with Solomon, Jeremiah and Timothy, but God helped these people in spite of their weaknesses, and he will help you as well.

You don't need to be an expert on the Bible or a trained teacher to lead a Bible discussion. The idea behind these inductive studies is that the leader guides group members to discover for themselves what the Bible has to say. This method of learning will allow group members to remember much more of what is said than a lecture would.

These studies are designed to be led easily. As a matter of fact, the flow of questions through the passage from observation to interpretation to application is so natural that you may feel that the studies lead themselves. This study guide is also flexible. You can use it with a variety of groups—student, professional, neighborhood or church groups. Each study takes forty-five to sixty minutes in a group setting.

There are some important facts to know about group dynamics and encouraging discussion. The suggestions listed below should enable you to effectively and enjoyably fulfill your role as leader.

PREPARING FOR THE STUDY

1. Ask God to help you understand and apply the passage in your own life. Unless this happens, you will not be prepared to lead others. Pray too for the various members of the group. Ask God to open your hearts to the message of his Word and motivate you to action.

2. Read the introduction to the entire guide to get an overview of the entire book and the issues which will be explored.

3. As you begin each study, read and reread the assigned Bible passage to familiarize yourself with it.

4. This study guide is based on the New Living Translation of the Bible. It will help you and the group if you use this translation as the basis for your study and discussion.

5. Carefully work through each question in the study. Spend time in meditation and reflection as you consider how to respond.

6. Write your thoughts and responses in the space provided in the study guide. This will help you to express your understanding of the passage clearly.

7. It might help to have a Bible dictionary handy. Use it to look up any unfamiliar words, names or places. (For additional help on how to study a passage, see chapter five of *How to Lead a LifeGuide Bible Study*, InterVarsity Press.)

8. Consider how you can apply the Scripture to your life. Remember that the group will follow your lead in responding to the studies. They will not go any deeper than you do.

9. Once you have finished your own study of the passage, familiarize yourself with the leader's notes for the study you are leading. These are designed to help you in several ways. First, they tell you the purpose the study guide author had in mind when writing the study. Take time to think through how the study questions work together to accomplish that purpose. Second, the notes provide you with additional background information or suggestions on group dynamics for various questions. This informa-

tion can be useful when people have difficulty understanding or answering a question. Third, the leader's notes can alert you to potential problems you may encounter during the study.

10. If you wish to remind yourself of anything mentioned in the leader's notes, make a note to yourself below that question in the study.

LEADING THE STUDY

1. Begin the study on time. Open with prayer, asking God to help the group to understand and apply the passage.

2. Be sure that everyone in your group has a study guide. Encourage the group to prepare beforehand for each discussion by reading the introduction to the guide and by working through the questions in the study.

3. At the beginning of your first time together, explain that these studies are meant to be discussions, not lectures. Encourage the members of the group to participate. However, do not put pressure on those who may be hesitant to speak during the first few sessions. You may want to suggest the following guidelines to your group.

   • Stick to the topic being discussed.

   • Your responses should be based on the verses that are the focus of the discussion and not on outside authorities such as commentaries or speakers.

   • Anything said in the group is considered confidential and will not be discussed outside the group unless specific permission is given to do so.

   • Listen attentively to each other and provide time for each person present to talk.

   • Pray for each other.

4. Play the DVD clip from the *Intimate Marriage DVD* and use the DVD reflection question to kick off group discussion. You can move directly from there to the beginning of the study section. Or, if you wish, you can also have a group member read the introduction aloud and then you can discuss the question in the "Open" section. If you do not have the DVD, then

be sure to kick off the discussion with the question in the "Open" section.

The "Open" question and the DVD clip are meant to be used before the passage is read. They introduce the theme of the study and encourage members to begin to open up. Encourage as many members as possible to participate, and be ready to get the discussion going with your own response.

This section is designed to reveal where your thoughts or feelings need to be transformed by Scripture. That is why it is especially important not to read the passage before the discussion question is asked. The passage will tend to color the honest reactions people would otherwise give because they are, of course, supposed to think the way the Bible does.

5. Have a group member (or members if the passage is long) read aloud the passage to be studied. Then give people several minutes to read the passage again silently so that they can take it all in.

6. Question 1 will generally be an overview question designed to briefly survey the passage. Encourage the group to look at the whole passage, but try to avoid getting sidetracked by questions or issues that will be addressed later in the study.

7. As you ask the questions, keep in mind that they are designed to be used just as they are written. You may simply read them aloud. Or you may prefer to express them in your own words.

There may be times when it is appropriate to deviate from the study guide. For example, a question may have already been answered. If so, move on to the next question. Or someone may raise an important question not covered in the guide. Take time to discuss it, but try to keep the group from going off on tangents.

8. The sidebars contain further background information on the texts in the study. If they are relevant to the course of your discussion, you may want to read them aloud. However, to keep the discussion moving, you may want to omit them and allow group members to read them on their own.

9. Avoid answering your own questions. If necessary, repeat or rephrase them until they are clearly understood. Or point out something you read in the

leader's notes to clarify the context or meaning. An eager group quickly becomes passive and silent if they think the leader will do most of the talking.

10. Don't be afraid of silence. People may need time to think about the question before formulating their answers.

11. Don't be content with just one answer. Ask, "What do the rest of you think?" or "Anything else?" until several people have given answers to the question.

12. Acknowledge all contributions. Try to be affirming whenever possible. Never reject an answer. If it is clearly off-base, ask, "Which verse led you to that conclusion?" or again, "What do the rest of you think?"

13. Don't expect every answer to be addressed to you, even though this will probably happen at first. As group members become more at ease, they will begin to truly interact with each other. This is one sign of healthy discussion.

14. Don't be afraid of controversy. It can be very stimulating. If you don't resolve an issue completely, don't be frustrated. Move on and keep it in mind for later. A subsequent study may solve the problem.

15. Periodically summarize what the group has said about the passage. This helps to draw together the various ideas mentioned and gives continuity to the study. But don't preach.

16. At the end of the Bible discussion, give couples an opportunity to discuss the "For the Couple" section and make the application personal. It's important to include this in your group time so that couples don't neglect discussing this material. Of course, sometimes couples may need to discuss the topic long beyond the five minutes of group time allotted, but you can help them get started in the meeting.

17. Encourage group members to work on the "Bonus" section between meetings as a couple or on their own. Give an opportunity during the session for people to talk about what they are learning.

18. End on time.

Many more suggestions and helps on leading a couples group are found in the *Intimate Marriage Leader's Guide*.

COMPONENTS OF SMALL GROUPS

A healthy small group should do more than study the Bible. There are four components to consider as you structure your time together.

Nurture. Small groups help us to grow in our knowledge and love of God. Bible study is the key to making this happen and is the foundation of your small group.

Community. Small groups are a great place to develop deep friendships with other Christians. Allow time for informal interaction before and after each study. Plan activities and games that will help you get to know each other. Spend time having fun together—going on a picnic or cooking dinner together.

Worship and prayer. Your study will be enhanced by spending time praising God together in prayer or song. Pray for each other's needs—and keep track of how God is answering prayer in your group. Ask God to help you to apply what you are learning in your study.

Outreach. Reaching out to others can be a practical way of applying what you are learning, and it will keep your group from becoming self-focused. Host a series of evangelistic discussions for your friends or neighbors. Clean up the yard of an elderly friend. Serve at a soup kitchen together, or spend a day working on a Habitat house.

Many more suggestions and helps in each of these areas are found in *Small Group Idea Book.* Information on building a small group can be found in *The Big Book on Small Groups* (both from InterVarsity Press). Reading through one of these books would be worth your time.

STUDY NOTES

Study 1. Family Traditions. Exodus 12:1-16; Matthew 26:17-30.

Purpose: To discover how traditions help create family bonds.

Question 1. The Passover remembers God's rescue of Israel from Egyptian slavery. They will soon begin the journey to the land that God promised to give the descendants of Abraham. The Lord's Supper, or Communion, is established for remembrance of the sacrifice of Jesus on the cross. His death and resurrection rescue his people from slavery to sin, guilt and death.

Question 2. Messianic Christians take great delight in celebrating Passover as a profound observance of *both* the Israelites' exodus and our redemption in Christ (see note to question 3). Participants in the study may have been involved in such seders, or they may have been Passover guests of non-Christian Jewish friends.

Question 3. The Last Supper which established Communion, and the death of Christ itself, took place during the Passover season. Jesus fulfills the exodus. He is our Passover lamb by his sacrifice.

Question 4. Family traditions are celebrations of some event in a family's past or of religious or cultural occasions. The Passover is clearly a family-oriented tradition, while the Lord's Supper is a church-based ritual. In this study we are not restricting ourselves to these two traditions but using them to discuss the value of traditions in general.

A family of two, husband and wife, can certainly establish and observe traditions.

Question 5. Traditions create and strengthen family bonds. A couple or larger family can look forward to them, participate in them together and remember them together. When connected to past events of redemption (Lord's Supper, Christmas, Easter, etc.), traditions can enhance spiritual maturity as they lead the family to reflect on the significance of the life, ministry and death of Christ.

If traditions become rote celebrations, done solely out of duty, then they can harm family unity and hinder spiritual growth. Jesus grew upset with the traditionalism of the Pharisees, for instance, because it did not come from a heart for God but reflected arrogance and lack of concern for the poor.

Question 6. Traditions described in the Bible are religious. But there is nothing wrong and everything proper about establishing other traditions that build family bonds. One example is New Year traditions. A family may seek to celebrate New Year's in a way that will allow them to reflect on the past year and look forward to the New Year. Such a tradition could be developed in a number of different ways, but the Christian family's reflections and hopes will not be divorced from their relationship with Jesus Christ. Another tradition that might strengthen a marriage is a periodic date night.

Question 7. This is not a question that allows for a simple yes or no answer. In biblical times the family was often assumed to be broader than the nuclear family of spouses and children. It would include parents, siblings, cousins and other relatives. On the other hand, the biblical text calls for a man to "leave[s] his father and mother" when getting married (Gen 2:24) and for a woman to do the same (Ps 45:10). Probably there should be some of both: traditions that involve the more immediate family and others involving the broader family. Questions like how and with whom Christmas will be celebrated are matters not of law but of wisdom.

Question 8. Participants may name religious events, seasonal transitions, personal days (anniversary, birthday) and other occasions that have special meaning (Memorial Day, Mother's Day, Father's Day). They might also do certain things on a weekly basis—like reading the Sunday paper together or going out for coffee on Saturday morning.

Bonus. The context makes it clear that sacrifice had become a "mere" tradition for Israel. That is, it was a matter of religious obligation, and sacrifices were not being offered with a passionate sense of sorrow for sin and gratitude for God's redemption. Further, God's people were making these sacrifices while seizing lands from the poor and practicing bribery and corruption.

Study 2. Family Stories. Deuteronomy 6:20-25; Psalm 78:1-8.

Purpose: To learn how we reveal our faith and ourselves to our spouse by telling each other stories about our past.

Question 1. They don't ask about the past. They ask about the law. The text doesn't really tell us why they are asking, but we can imagine that they are curious about the reason they are to act a certain way. Today our children often ask similar questions. "Why do we have to go to church?" "Why do we do this? Other families don't." Such questions will stimulate the telling of our stories of redemption.

Question 2. They respond by telling the story of God's salvation. God saved them from bondage in Egypt, and so they respond by obeying him. Since he saved them, they know he has their best interests at heart. On this basis they can believe that the law also is provided with their best interests in mind.

Question 4. Perhaps verse 7 says it best: "So each generation can set its hope anew on God, remembering his glorious miracles and obeying his commands."

Question 5. In the Old Testament God chose a nation, constituted by tribes and the tribes by families, to be his people. Thus it made sense that the primary location for the passing on of faith stories was the family. However, in the New Testament God's people come from many nations and many families. Yet when a married couple share faith, the family again becomes the first place where stories of faith are told. Together they go to church and share their stories with others.

Question 6. Stories of faith first of all include the accounts of Christ's winning our redemption. This will lead us to read and study Scripture together. But they are also stories of how God is acting in our lives—in other words, the application of redemption.

Stories of hope are about our dreams and desires. When we allow ourselves to speak about the future, we are telling a story of hope.

Stories of love are centered on sacrifice and care. Such stories reveal the courage necessary to give and receive compassion and intimacy in a world where love seems fleeting and unsure.

Question 7. When we hear what Christ has done for others and how he has worked in other people's lives, it encourages us to live with confidence (faith), hope and love. It also encourages us to be observant and expectant that God is going to continue to work in our life.

Question 8. These stories come from the Scripture and from our lives. We become familiar with the stories of Scripture through frequent reading and study of the Bible, alone and together. We discern the stories of God's intervention in our lives through being alert to see the hand of God in circumstances, relationships, answers to prayer. We also learn stories by listening to other believers who tell of God's work in their lives.

Study 3. Family Traumas. 2 Samuel 12:1-16; Philippians 3:12-14.

Purpose: To recognize and grapple with the effects of past family sin on present relationships.

Question 1. In the first place, it reminds us that David was a king, a powerful person who was potentially dangerous, even for a prophet like Nathan. Perhaps even more, it shows that we deceive ourselves about our sin. David may not have recognized just how bad he was until he heard the story of the rich man stealing a sheep from a poor person. After all, he was king, and kings of the ancient Near East usually assumed they could have any woman and kill any man they wanted. David of course knew better when he thought about it, but his power may have gone to his head. The fact that he was not leading his army in battle as he should have been (2 Sam 11:1) already indicates that he is shirking his responsibilities.

Question 2. God will make sure that there are negative consequences to David's sin (2 Sam 12:11-12). His own children will rebel against him, and his wives will be taken by another man. The fulfillment of this judgment comes most pointedly when his son Absalom leads a rebellion against him and in the process sleeps with David's concubines publicly (2 Sam 16:21-22).

Opinions will differ over whether this is fair. Some will argue that since it is God's judgment, it is by definition fair. Others will think God is harsh here. The point of the passage is clear, though, and conforms with the broader teaching of Scripture that sin has negative consequences. One could argue that it would not be fair if David simply walked away unscathed, particularly after heartlessly having Uriah killed.

Question 3. Repentance does not wipe the slate clean in terms of consequences. Certainly the negative effects of sin continue in David's and his children's lives. However, repentance does restore relationship with God and provides hope for the future. To not repent would lead to even more dire consequences.

Question 4. We think we can get away with it. We try to deny that our sins will affect us or our children. And indeed we may be able to avoid the immediate consequences of our sin; this only encourages further bad behavior.

Question 5. Observation and study have shown that children of alcoholics will struggle in particular ways, as will the offspring of abusers. The list could go on. Nonetheless, as the next question reminds us, the situation is far from hopeless.

Question 6. Paul says he does not look back at the past. His past involved sinful persecution of the church, so much so that he considered himself the "chief of all sinners" (1 Tim 1:15). But his eyes are on Christ. That this involves present struggle is clear from the passage, but the message is clear: there is hope that the damage of the past can be broken in the present and the future.

Question 7. In the first place, Paul is saying that he is in the process of forgetting and that it is a struggle. But as long as he keeps his focus on Christ and the future, he is moving in the right direction.

Yet we should be clear about what forgetting and remembering mean in the Bible. It is not just a matter of whether we can recall a past event. The important thing is whether we behave in a way that conforms to the remembrance. To remember God in Scripture does not mean simply to have God in mind; it means to serve him. We can forget God even while thinking about him if our thinking about him does not lead to worship. Thus to forget the past means not acting in a way that is affected by the past, not allowing the past to determine our enjoyment of the present.

Bonus. The answer to this question will bring a variety of answers, but included among these might be physical and sexual abuse, alcoholism, neglect, the death of a sibling or a parent.

Study 4. Family Comparisons. Genesis 37:2-8.

Purpose: To be aware of how family dynamics are affecting your children and your marriage.

Question 3. Our relationships with our children should be second most important, after our relationship with our spouse. Thus how we relate as individuals and as a couple to our children can be the cause of both great joy and great friction in our marriage. Differences over treatment of children can create huge problems in a marriage.

Question 4. All our children are equally deserving of our love and concern. It may be that one child needs more attention than another at a certain time. But parents should be very careful to make sure that the other children are aware of their love and the reason they are focusing extra time and energy on this child.

Question 5. Even when parents are particularly careful to treat their children equally, children will often jockey for power. Competition seems to be particularly strong among boys who are close in age. It is the rare family that never has to deal with these issues.

Question 6. Children will often try to play parents off one another. Also, husbands and wives frequently have different expectations of their children and different ideas about how to handle problems. These differences may lead to conflict. What is most tragic is when a parent uses a child against the other parent. Often children are the battleground of marriage wars. This is diabolic and must be addressed with a competent counselor to break a dark and damaging pattern.

Question 7. In the first place, parents should do their best to assure the children of their equal love for them. They should discipline them in love, not out of anger. They should also let their children know that they are important to them, but not as important as their spouse.

The married couple should talk and pray together about the best strategy for raising their children. They should listen well to each other. In the final analysis, parents must remember that their children are in God's hands. This will keep parents from panicking and seeking to exert unhealthy control over their children's lives.

Question 8. This scenario is difficult. There is no formula (like "Dad always makes the final decision") that will allow for easy resolution of all such conflicts. The couple must continue to discuss matters and be open to each other. They should not allow the disagreement to fracture their relationship. Ultimately they should trust God and pray that he will guide them to the right decision. Compromise may be necessary.

Bonus. Forgiveness leads to this new situation. Joseph does not seek revenge, but rather, he offers forgiveness because he sees God's hand rather than his brother's hatred behind his hard life. On the other hand, the brothers are able to be close to Joseph because he offers them this type of forgiveness.

Study 5. Family Legalism. Colossians 2:14-23.

Purpose: To discover how the creation of requirements beyond God's law stifles spiritual and relational growth.

Question 1. Paul argues that these rules prohibiting certain foods and drinks and requiring certain observances of special days are not divinely sanctioned laws but rather laws imposed by other human beings.

Question 2. There are laws that still direct our action and thinking as Christians. Jesus told us as much in the Sermon on the Mount (Mt 5:17-20); in fact, Jesus emphasized and intensified the law for Christians. Not only are we not to murder, we are not to hate. Not only are we not to commit adultery, we are not to lust. Legalism is not the observance of divinely given law; it is insistence on laws not found in the Bible, or the belief that we are saved by our observance of laws.

Question 3. These situations do not come under law but are matters of wisdom, depending on the circumstance. Rightness or wrongness depends on the timing and other conditions. It may be necessary for a husband to work that hard for a limited period of time. There is no law that a person cannot work that hard. Then again, it might be a sign of workaholism. The wife may have a good explanation for spending time with another man; if so, she will be able to give the proper assurances to her husband that nothing untoward is going on. There is no law that a married woman can't spend time with other men. Requiring that a child look before crossing the street is an appropriate family rule to protect his or her safety.

Question 4. Among the different types of writings in the Bible are Law (the Ten Commandments are the best example) and Wisdom (see the book of Proverbs as an example), both of which seek to direct God's people on how to live. There is an important difference between the two. Law is always operative. It is never right to murder, never right to commit adultery. Wisdom is sensitive to time and circumstance. Sometimes it is best to "answer a fool," sometimes better "not to answer" (see Prov 26:4-5). It depends on the situation.

The Bible tells us what God demands. True, sometimes it is not immediately clear what laws from the Old Testament are still relevant to modern life and how they are to apply, but the principle is that law must be derived from the Bible. Wisdom depends on the circumstance and is more like advice than like demand.

Question 5. There is no formula for wisdom. However, the foundation is constant study of Scripture, in particular a book like Proverbs, to get perspective on how to live and principles for navigating life well. Then it is important to observe and learn from life around us. It's easy to see that it is dangerous to cross a road without looking both ways. To preserve the life of our children, we will teach them to look before crossing. It doesn't take long to figure out that if a husband and wife don't spend any time alone together, their marriage begins to wilt on the vine. So though it would be wrong to establish "We must spend an hour a day together alone" as an inviolable law, it certainly is advice that can help build a healthy marriage.

Question 6. Legalism typically leads to either repression or rebellion. Out of a parent's appropriate desire to protect a daughter from having illicit sexual relations before marriage, he or she may be tempted toward a repressive approach, telling the daughter, "No kissing or touching before marriage." This girl may then either rebel by becoming promiscuous or be so frightened of sex that she has difficulty expressing her sexuality even in marriage.

Question 7. Attempts to fence the law may spring from devotion, but underneath there is always fear and a desire to control. It is actually easier to practice a religion in which expectations are spelled out in detail. We are often afraid of true freedom.

Question 9. If a husband and wife are properly submitting to each other out of love, putting each other's agenda ahead of their own, it will never get to this point. But if a husband is staying out late at night and coming home drunk, then a wife can put a demand on him, because getting drunk is forbidden in Scripture. If a wife is beating the children, a husband can insist that she stop. But again, the principle underlying healthy marriages is mutual submission.

Study 6. A Spiritual Legacy. Selections from Proverbs.

Purpose: To explore the power of spiritual legacy.

Question 1. In this proverb and throughout the book, the assumption is that children left to their own devices will stay foolish.

Question 2. Discipline means an enforced directing of the energy and behavior of a child. This verse does not specify the nature of the discipline. It can include determined teaching, rewards and punishments, and even lovingly applied physical punishment (see Prov 13:24; 23:13-14). The method of discipline depends a lot on the child.

Question 3. The "right path" is defined by the rest of the book of Proverbs and indeed the whole Bible. It is the way that God wants us to go. It is the way of godliness, righteousness, fairness, obedience.

Question 4. They are blessed because they have wonderful role models in their godly parents.

Question 5. The proverb features what is called an antithetical parallelism, stating the same truth from two opposite perspectives. It says that evil people will be punished for their wrongdoing. The second part implies that not only will good people be blessed, but their children will also benefit from their integrity.

Question 6. Proverbs do not invariably hold true (see study note 4 in study 5, on law and wisdom). A proverb like this assumes a godly family. A godly grandparent finds joy in a godly grandchild. A godly child finds joy in the previous generations. This proverb is an ideal we are to strive toward.

Question 7. According to Proverbs 2, we are to work hard to get wisdom and godliness. But when we do, we should thank God for the gift of wisdom. It seems paradoxical, and indeed it is. But we need to do both, work hard and respond in gratitude.